I0711263
This Dogs Coloring Book
Belongs To :

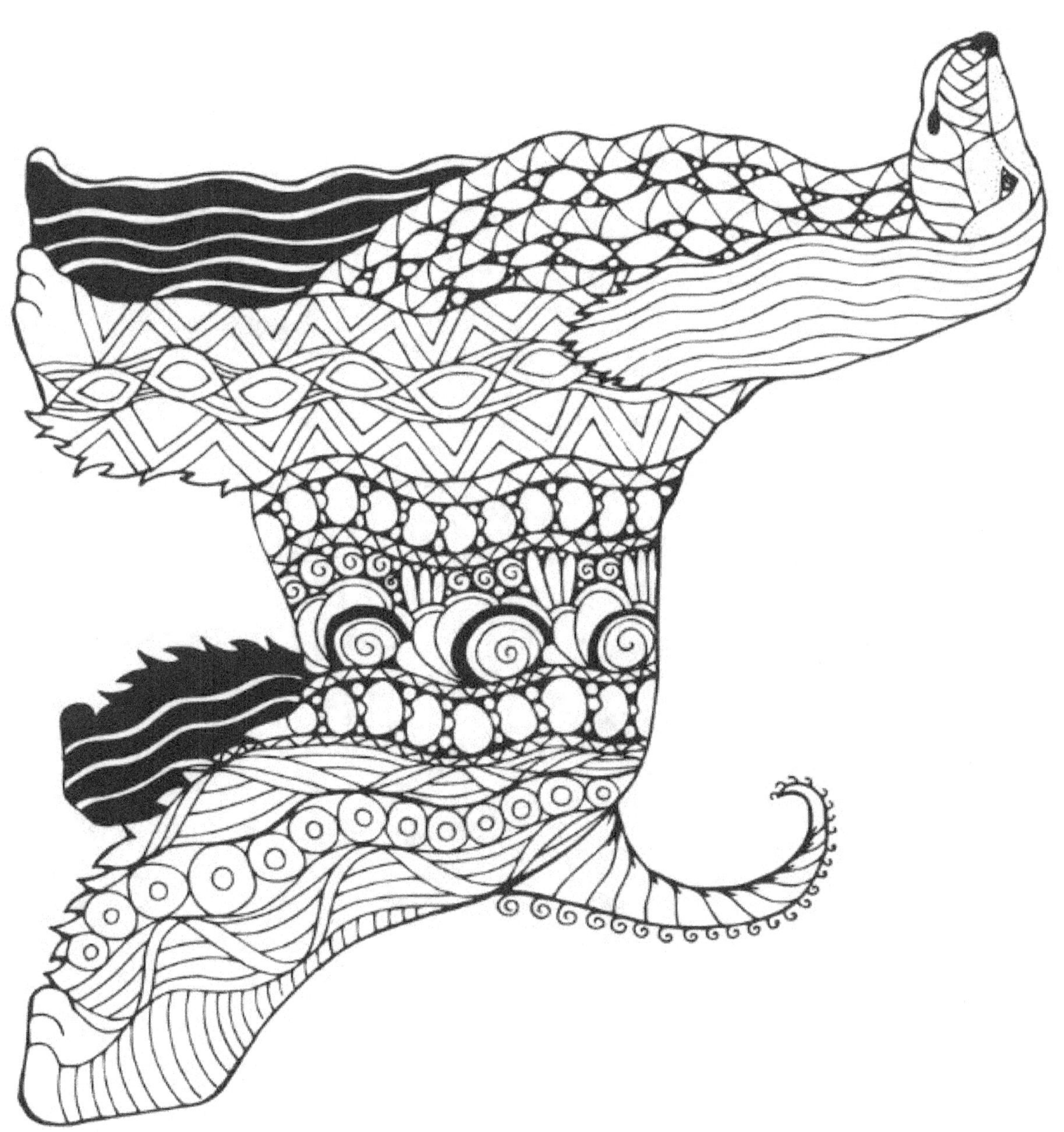

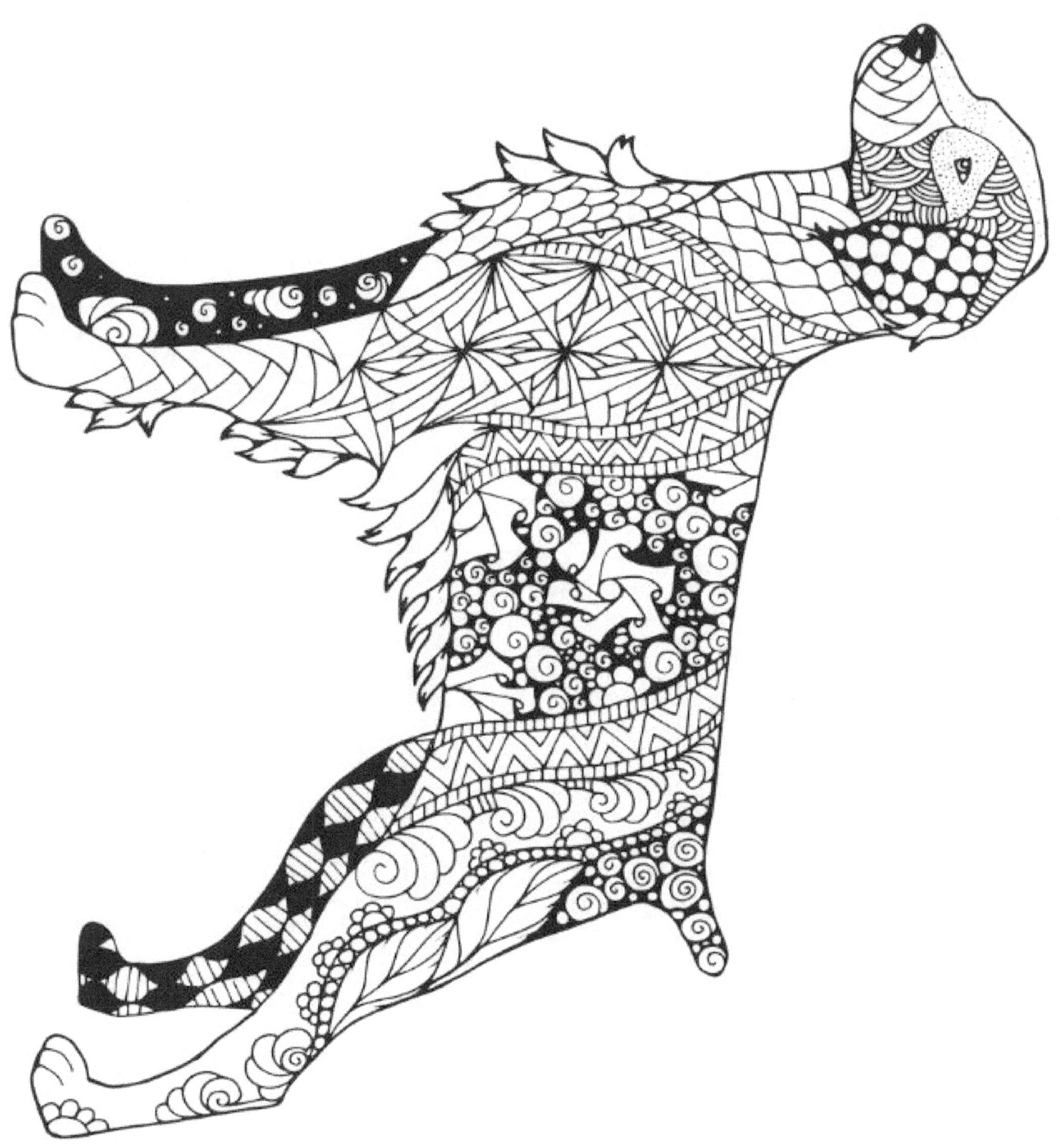

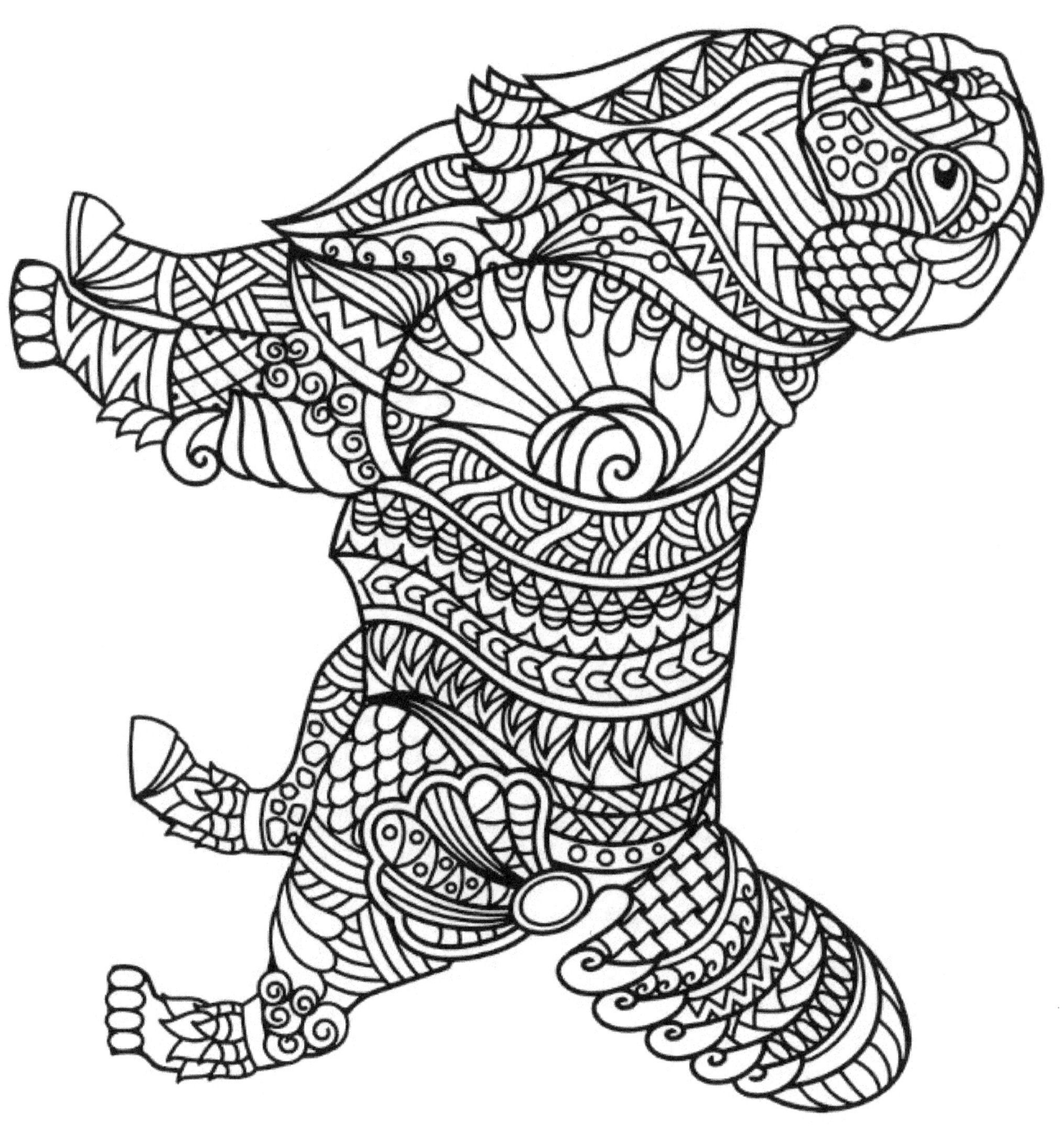

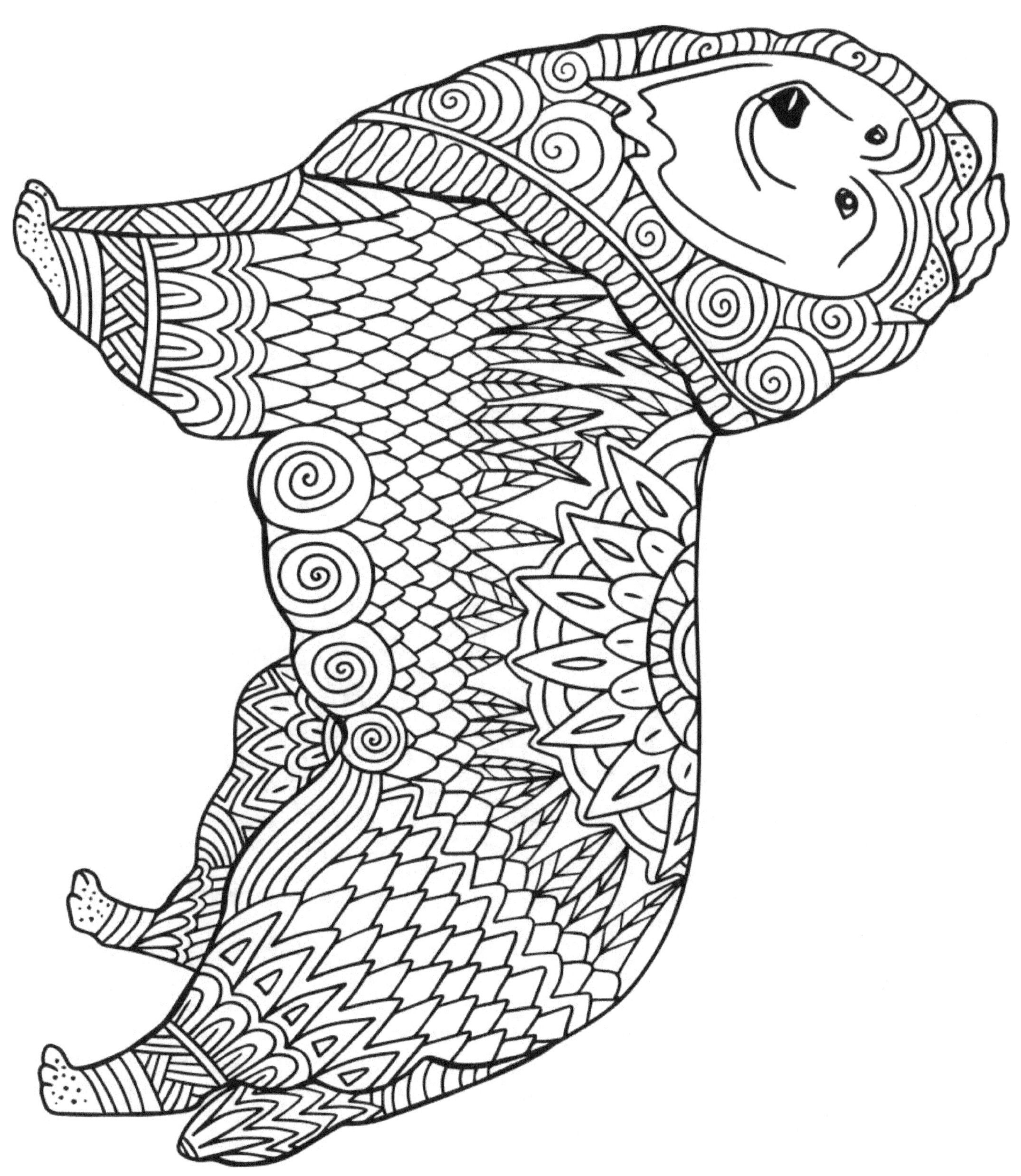

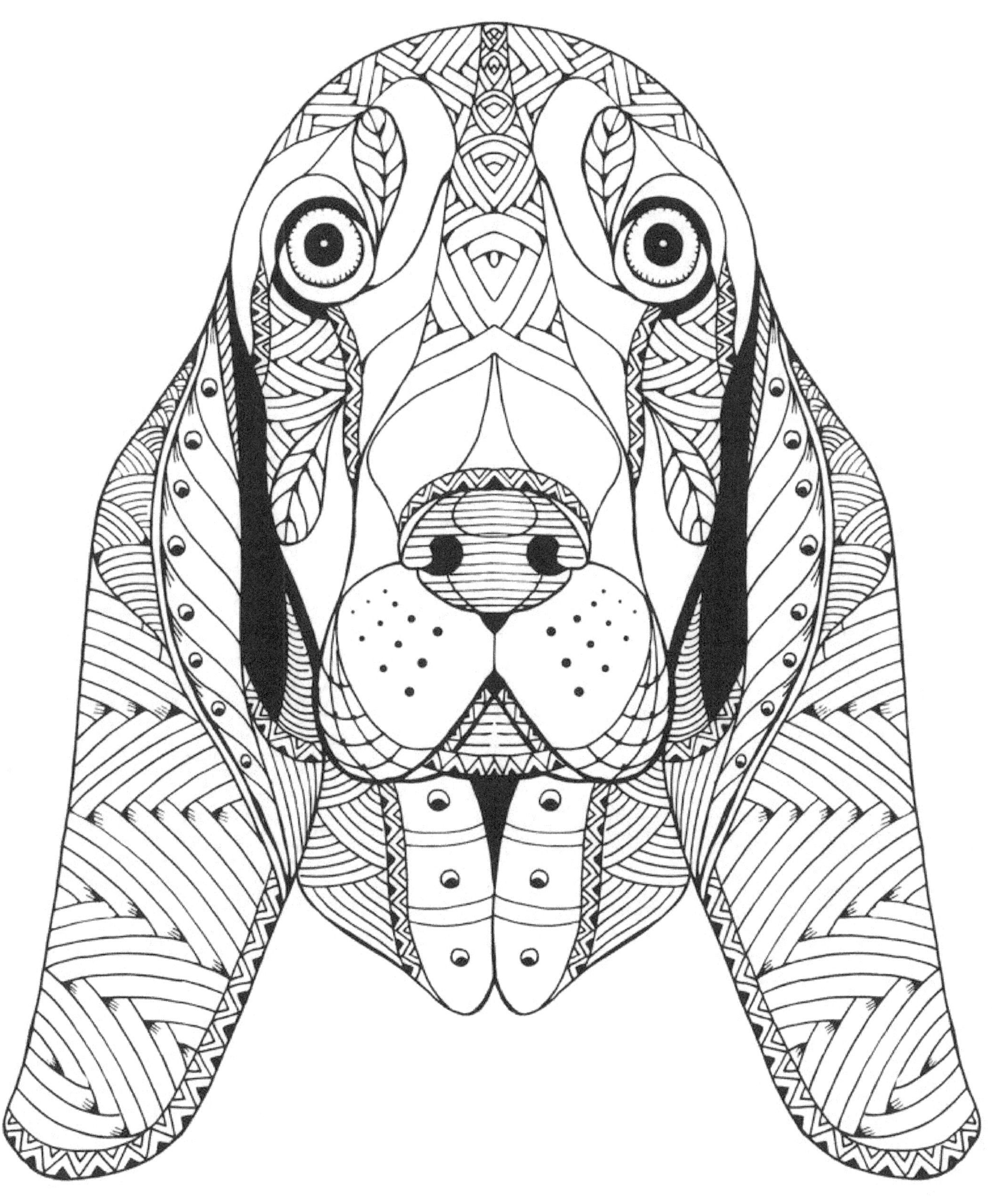

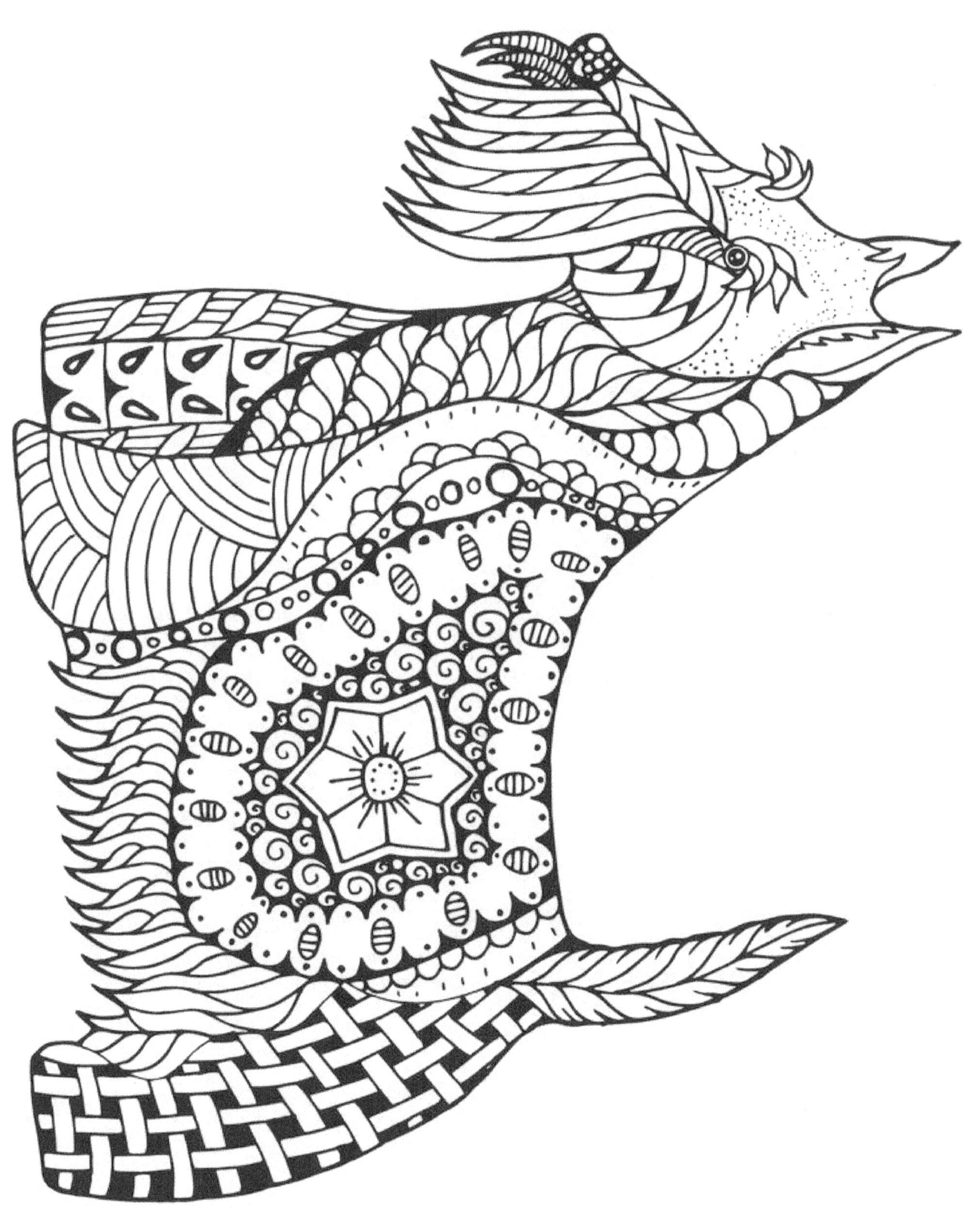

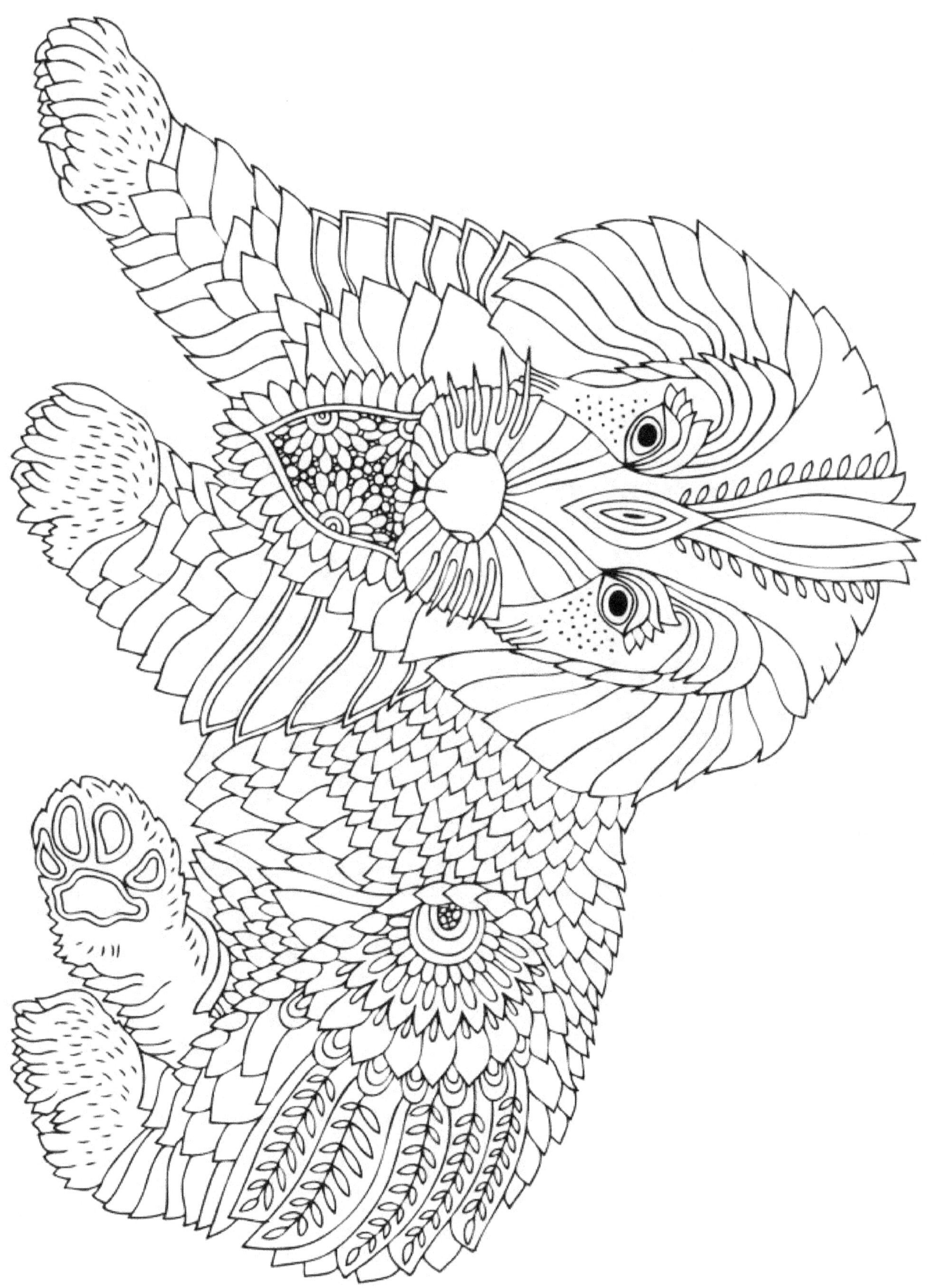

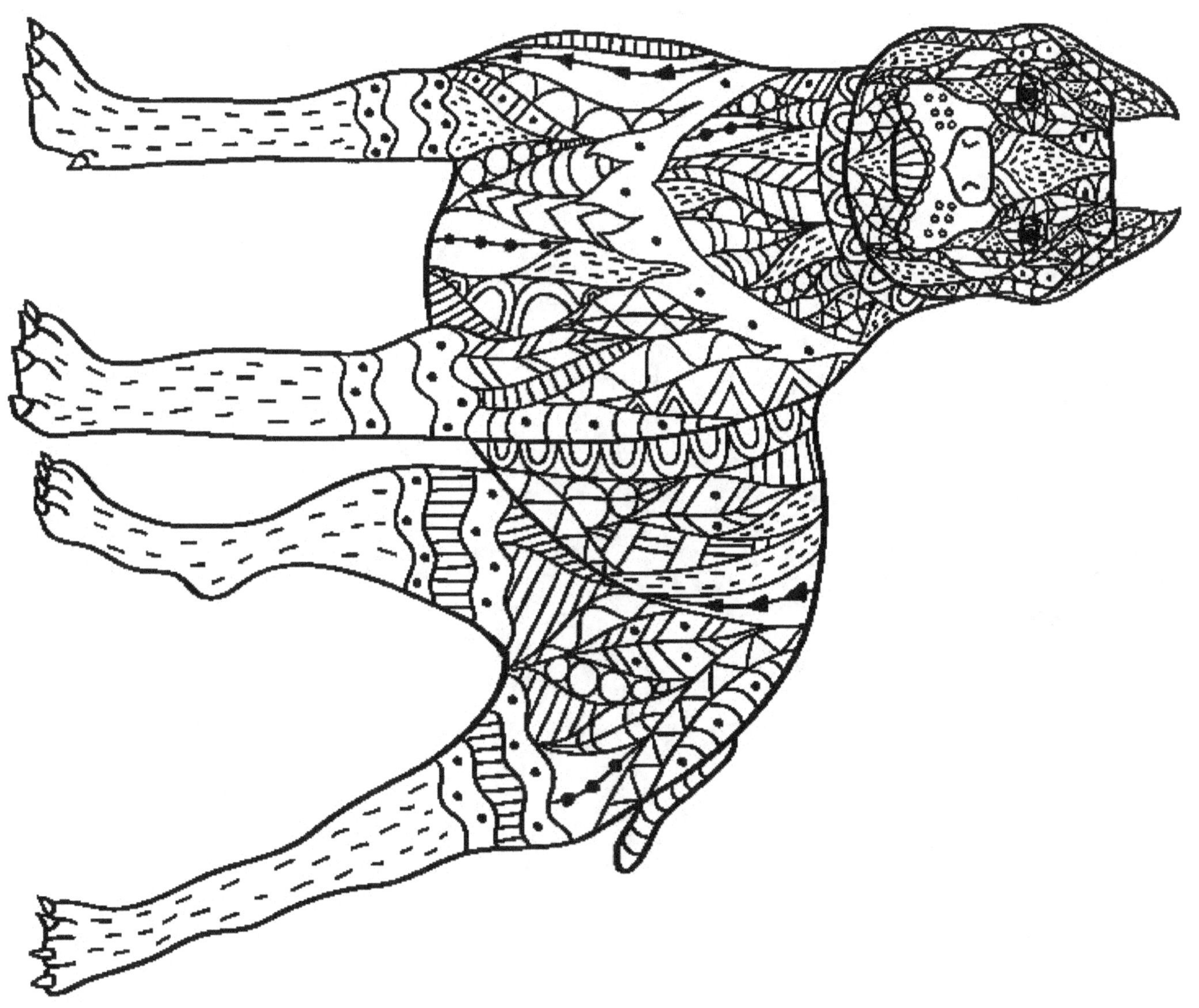

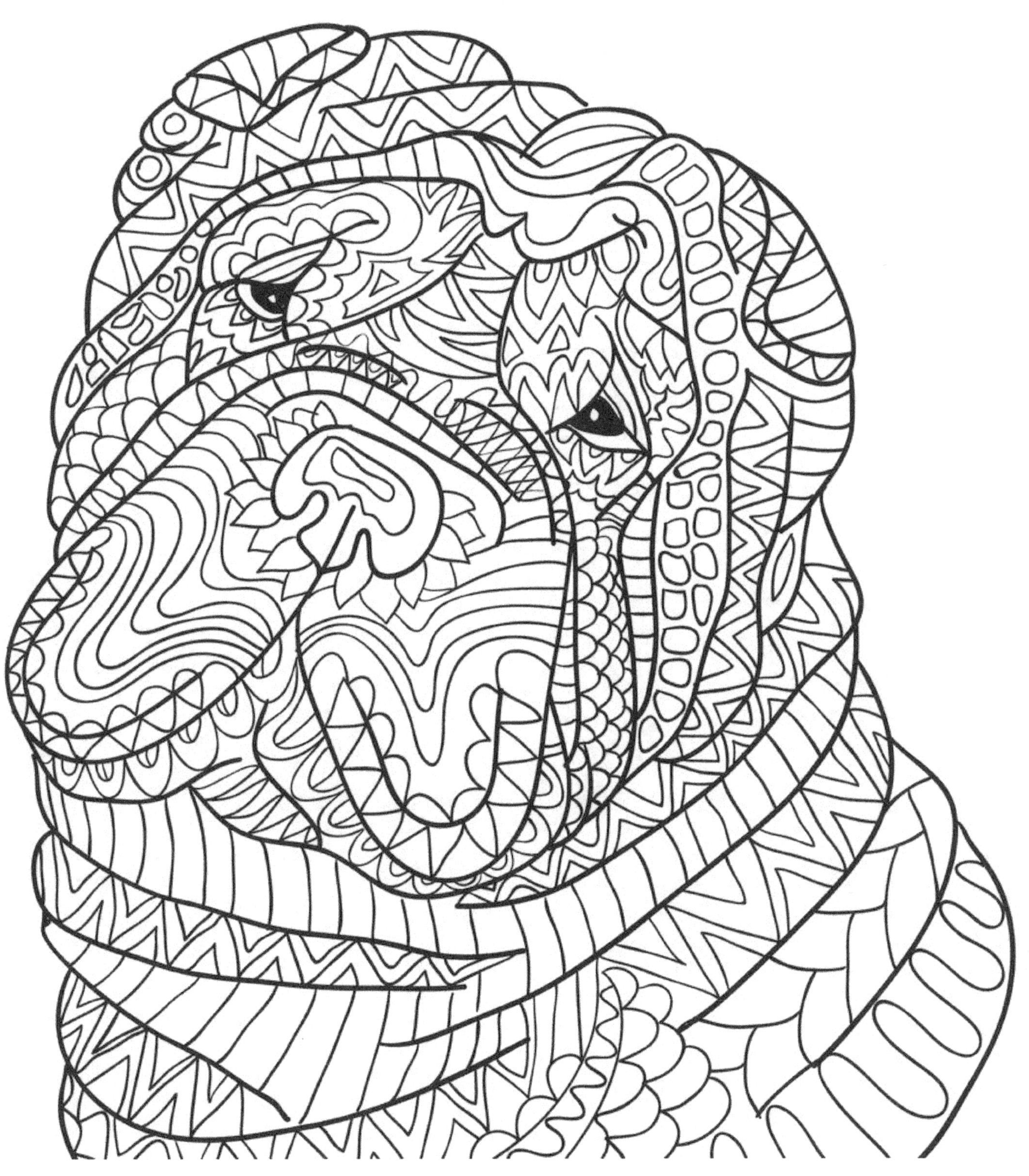